MALACHI DADS

PSALM

1

THE BLESSED MAN

D1411998

MALACHI DADS

PSALM 1

THE BLESSED MAN

BY MALACHI DADS AT THE LOUISIANA STATE PENITENTIARY AT ANGOLA

LIFELINE
GLOBAL™

lifelineglobal.org

© 2014

3 4 5 6 19 18 17

Psalm 1:1-6 — *Blessed is the man who walks not in the counsel of the wicked, nor stands in the way of sinners, nor sits in the seat of scoffers; but his delight is in the law of the LORD, and on His law he meditates day and night. He is like a tree planted by streams of water that yields its fruit in its season, and its leaf does not wither. In all that he does, he prospers. The wicked are not so, but are like chaff that the wind drives away. Therefore the wicked will not stand in the judgment, nor sinners in the congregation of the righteous; for the LORD knows the way of the righteous, but the way of the wicked will perish.*

FOREWORD

FOREWORD

In writing this foreword for *Psalm 1: The Blessed Man* I can't help but think of Awana Co-founder Art Rorheim. When I first met him, I knew immediately Mr. Rorheim was a great man of God. He wanted the inmates to memorize Scripture — said it would be good for them. I thought, *These are grown men and they probably won't be interested.* Mr. Art, as I called him, immediately started quoting Psalm 1 and the first verse is *Blessed is the man that walketh not in the counsel of the ungodly* ... (KJV). I knew then he was right. If I could get prisoners to learn and live Psalm 1, I would have a safer prison. The inmates' culture of every man for himself would change. Psalm 1 could be the catalyst, along with the seminary, for true rehabilitation — moral rehabilitation.

Today, after many men spent hours memorizing God's Word starting with Psalm 1 and quoting Scripture, the change has occurred. Moral rehabilitation began changing the prison culture, exceeding all our expectations. Psalm 1 inspired the prisoners to live godly lives and it can change you. It was an honor and blessing to have God send Art Rorheim to Angola via Manny Mill to touch prisoners all over the world, memorizing Scripture and mentoring their children through Malachi Dads™ and Returning Hearts™.

Burl Cain
Warden (Retired), Louisiana State Penitentiary at Angola

God's Word changes lives! *Psalm 1: The Blessed Man* is an introductory book (including Bible study and Scripture memory) to our Malachi Dads Bible studies, which are each 12 weeks long.

We believe the short *Psalm 1: The Blessed Man Bible* studies will help prepare you for your journey of life transformation around God's Word.

At Lifeline Gobal Ministries™ we believe Psalm 119:9-11: *How can a young man keep his way pure? By guarding it according to Your word. With my whole heart I seek You; let me not wander from Your commandments! I have stored up Your word in my heart, that I might not sin against You.*

As you begin this journey of following Christ, our prayer is for you to experience a godly lifestyle that deeply impacts and changes you to be a Christ-follower all the days of your life. We pray that it impacts you to become a godly influence, godly husband, and godly father. We believe as God's Word changes you, as a father you will also impact your children for good and share the gospel of Jesus Christ with them!

Grace to you,

Mike Broyles
Executive Director
Lifeline Global Ministries™

INTRODUCTION

On a scale of one to 10, how would you rate your life? A decade ago I would have said a one. I was considered a **cursed** man, a wicked man. Nothing — and I mean absolutely nothing — was going right for me. I didn't know the Lord. I was a man who loved evil. That all changed when I trusted Jesus. I became a **blessed** man. I went from being a man who was a taker to a giver, a man who had NO family and friends to a man who had more than enough, a man with no purpose to a man who helps others discover and fulfill their purpose.

Everyone has a desire to be **blessed**. We all want to live a prosperous and successful life, one where we are satisfied and content in every area of our lives. The Bible serves as an example for us of how to live a life glorifying to God. It is filled with the true stories of men and women of God who lived their lives so well that they deserved to be mentioned in the Bible.

Is it still possible to be blessed in a wicked and perverse world? The answer is absolutely yes! Yes, you can be blessed. The Word of God is the key. This study will help you begin your journey to being blessed.

Let's look at a very familiar passage of Scripture:

Deuteronomy 30:19-20 — *I call heaven and earth to witness against you today, that I have set before you life and death, blessing and curse. Therefore choose life, that you and your offspring may live, loving the LORD your God, obeying His* *voice and holding fast to Him, for He is your life and length of days, that you may dwell in the land that the LORD swore to your fathers, to Abraham, to Isaac, and to Jacob, to give them.*

Those two verses are powerful. God is talking to His chosen people, Israel. Notice in those verses the blessing was something that was theirs if they **obeyed**. The same way God promised to bless His people if they obeyed His Word, He still promises to bless us if we obey. Likewise, God promises to curse those who disobey.

Don't you love **tests** that come from God? He gives you the question and then tells you the answer. The same principle applies today that applied back then. We have the option to obey the Word of God and be blessed or disobey Him and be cursed.

WHAT IS THE KEY TO BEING BLESSED?

Key Note: Being a born-again believer is the most important thing in this world to be. It means you belong to God. It means you are headed to heaven. Being a born-again believer is the first and most important step in becoming a **blessed** man. But it is more than that. In order to experience the fullness of being a born-again believer, you must *know* the Word of God and *do* the Word of God. The key is **obeying**.

James 1:21-22 — *Therefore put away all filthiness and rampant wickedness and receive with meekness the implanted word, which is able to save your souls. But be doers of the word, and not hearers only, deceiving yourselves.*

In his epistle, James told the believers what they needed to do in order to experience the fullness of the Word. Not only did they have to *hear* the Word, but they had to *do* the Word.

The same is true today. We must do the Word in order to experience the fullness of what it means to be blessed. You must **hear** the Word and **do** the Word of God. If the key is obeying, we must learn the Word. The way to learn the Word of God is not necessarily just by reading it. The key is to **memorize** God's Word.

Do you have any passages of Scripture **memorized**? If so, write them down on the lines provided below. If you don't have any Scriptures memorized, explain what it is you believe you need to do in order to start memorizing Scripture.

_____

_____

_____

_____

There are several methods that can be used in order to memorize Scripture. **Repetition** is one of the most effective methods. According to Awana® Co-founder Art Rorheim, repetition is the key to memorizing Scripture. The method requires you to recite the passage over and over. Once you have repeated it over and over, _do it again_.

The practice of memorizing Scripture is biblically based. When Satan tempted Jesus in Matthew 4, Jesus rebuked him with Scripture. He was armed with the Word, and we must also be in order to have victory in our day-to-day lives. The key to being prepared and armed with the Word is to **memorize** it.

To help us in our quest to learn how to **memorize** Scripture, we will take one of the most famous chapters in the entire Bible — Psalm 1 — and break it down, piece by piece.

We will look at the passage and discover just how simple and easy it is to be a **blessed** man. If you can get the Word hidden in your heart, you will be armed with the Word. If you begin to live by the Word, you will be blessed by God. The key to being blessed is simple: **obey God's Word.**

THROUGH CHRIST I CAN.

Philippians 4:13 — *I can do all things through Him who strengthens me.*

When I first was introduced to the challenge of memorizing Psalm 1:1-6, I didn't believe I could do it. I was used to memorizing one Scripture verse at a time. But I went to a church call-out one night and the pastor asked the whole congregation to stand up and recite the passage. At first, I said to myself: "They aren't all going to say those verses!" But to my amazement, they did. The young and the old all knew Psalm 1. I felt out of place to be one of the only ones in the church who didn't know it.

I went to my dorm and I made a commitment to learn that passage of Scripture. I read it over and over and over again. To my surprise, I was able to memorize it in four days. I felt so proud of myself. I felt joyful because I had really accomplished something.

The next time they had church and the pastor got up and asked everyone to recite the Psalm passage, I was able to boldly and confidently recite it.

I have been able to memorize other chapters of the Bible since then. My life is changing because of it. Whenever I have to make a decision, certain Scriptures come to mind and I am able to make better choices. I have also been able to challenge my family with Scripture memorization. They memorize different passages because I do. *Wherever the head goes, the body will follow …*

Inmate John N.

INTRODUCTION

THE BLESSED MAN *DOES NOT* FELLOWSHIP WITH THE WICKED.

READ PSALM 1:1-6.

Psalm 1 — *Blessed is the man who walks not in the counsel of the wicked, nor stands in the way of sinners, nor sits in the seat of scoffers*; but his delight is in the law of the LORD, and on His law he meditates day and night. He is like a tree planted by streams of water that yields its fruit in its season, and its leaf does not wither. In all that he does, he prospers. The wicked are not so, but are like chaff that the wind drives away. Therefore the wicked will not stand in the judgment, nor sinners in the congregation of the righteous; for the LORD knows the way of the righteous, but the way of the wicked will perish.

In the first week of our study, we will look at something that the blessed man **does not** do. The blessed man does not keep company with the wicked.

Verse 1: *Blessed is the man who walks not in the counsel of the wicked, nor stands in the way of sinners, nor sits in the seat of scoffers.*

What does it mean to be blessed? _____

_____

_____

Key Word: Blessed (*barak*). The word *barak* is mentioned 26 times in the book of Psalms. When it is used in reference to God, it means "to praise." However, when it is used in reference to man it means "happy."

Many people have a misconception of what it means to be blessed. Some people believe that to have a lot of money means they are blessed. Some people believe that if they have a lot of stuff they are blessed. The list goes on. That is not true. You can have a lot of money and a lot of things and still be *miserable*. Therefore, material things do not mean you are blessed.

What does it mean to be wicked? _____

_____

_____

What makes a person wicked is their heart. It's a big difference from being a Christian who is in the process of being conformed to the image of Christ and a person who is simply without Christ. The author of Psalm 1 is referring to a person who is not in covenant with God. All throughout the Bible, God makes it very clear that His chosen people are not to keep company with the ungodly.

Describe some of the problems a person can experience from being in the presence of sinners. _____

_____

_____

_____

The first verse of this passage teaches us one of the ways to be blessed. The author starts off by conveying the importance of not being in the presence of evil. Often the company we keep can get us in trouble.

Are there people currently in your life you need to remove? If so, pray and ask God to give you the strength to remove them.

MEMORY SCRIPTURES:

Psalm 1:1: *Blessed is the man who walks not in the counsel of the wicked, nor stands in the way of sinners, nor sits in the seat of scoffers.*

1 Corinthians 15:33: *Do not be deceived: "Bad company ruins good morals."*

CONCLUSION:

In the first verse of the Psalm 1 passage, we learned that one of the keys to being blessed is to avoid keeping company with the wicked.

HOMEWORK ASSIGNMENT:

A failure to plan is a plan to fail. For this week's homework, explain what you will do the next time those people who aren't good for your life come to you and want to commune with you. Spend time memorizing **verse 1** of Psalm 1.

I CHOOSE JESUS.

My friends were my life. We ate together, hung out together, and did everything together. When I came to know the Lord Jesus and I started reading the Bible, I encountered Psalm 1. I knew my friends were not righteous. They were wicked. I knew I was a Christian, but I didn't immediately see my friends as a hindrance to me. I started to see clearly they were headed one way and I was headed another way. I would go to church and they would play basketball. I would read my Bible, they would read rap magazines. Even so, I kept telling myself that they were my friends.

One night when I was on my way to church, I was tempted to join them at the gym to play basketball. But I didn't go. I knew that I had to break away from that negative crowd. And, man-oh-man, I am glad I did. That night they all got in serious trouble, and I didn't because I wasn't there. I praised God for that.

This encounter opened my eyes up to a harsh reality. Darkness and light do not have anything to do with each other. I now realize the best thing for me to do for my friends is to pray for them and to witness to them through my lifestyle. No matter what may happen, I choose Jesus.

Inmate Daniel R.

WEEK 1

THE BLESSED MAN *DELIGHTS* IN THE LORD.

READ PSALM 1:1-6.

Psalm 1 — *Blessed is the man who walks not in the counsel of the wicked, nor stands in the way of sinners, nor sits in the seat of scoffers;* **but his delight is in the law of the LORD, and on His law he meditates day and night.** *He is like a tree planted by streams of water that yields its fruit in its season, and its leaf does not wither. In all that he does, he prospers. The wicked are not so, but are like chaff that the wind drives away. Therefore the wicked will not stand in the judgment, nor sinners in the congregation of the righteous; for the LORD knows the way of the righteous, but the way of the wicked will perish.*

This week we will spend time on verse 2 of Psalm 1. In this verse we will look at something that a blessed man **does**. The blessed man **delights** in the law of the Lord.

Verse 2: *But his delight is in the law of the LORD, and on His law he meditates day and night.*

According to Psalm 1:2, the blessed man delights in the law of the Lord. The law of the Lord during this time was abiding by the commandments and statues which were found in the law of Moses. This is the key: delighting in the law of the Lord.

Describe what the word *delight* means to you. _____

_____

_____

It is the things we delight in that we have a tendency to do. List five things that you delight in.

1. _____

2. _____

3. _____

4. _____

5. _____

In the latter part of verse 2 of this passage, the psalmist describes how delighting in the law of God looks. When he wrote *meditates day and night*, he was describing what it means to delight in the law of the Lord.

What does it mean to meditate on something? _____

_____

_____

To meditate on the Word of God simply means to keep it on your mind, to continue to look at, dwell on, and pay attention to it.

What happens when a person meditates on something? _____

_____

_____

What we meditate on, we do. What we mediate on, we become.

There is a difference between reading the law of the Lord and meditating on the law of the Lord. The psalmist is very clear, the blessed man meditates on the law **day** and **night**.

MEMORY SCRIPTURES:

Psalm 1:2: *But his delight is in the law of the LORD, and on His law he meditates day and night.*

Joshua 1:8: *This Book of the Law shall not depart from your mouth, but you shall meditate on it day and night, so that you may be careful to do according to all that is written in it. For then you will make your way prosperous, and then you will have good success.*

HOMEWORK:

This week journal the amount of time you spend each day meditating on the Bible. Be ready to present your journal in the next class. Spend some time memorizing verse 2 of Psalm 1.

I NEVER KNEW.

I had heard a few people talk about delighting in the Word of God and how it made them feel. But I didn't really believe it. I challenged myself to do it and to my surprise, *it was like nothing I have ever experienced.* When I found myself delighting in the law of the Lord, I experienced peace. I didn't and couldn't focus on anything but just how awesome God is. My faith was strengthened and I felt better about everything. I knew God was in control.

I have learned very quickly that when you meditate on the Word of God, delightfulness automatically comes along with it. It's like the world stops and all the burdens are lifted and everything is calm. I started mediating on the Word of God so much until I would dream about reading the Bible in my dreams. And the joy and peace I have when I meditate on the Word of God is indescribable. It's like nothing I have encountered. I am physically in prison, but *I am not in prison. I am in God.* My prayer is that every believer will learn the benefits of meditating on the Word of God. Truly the Word is my new-found delight.

Inmate Troy D.

WEEK 3

THE DESCRIPTION OF THE *BLESSED* MAN

READ PSALM 1:1-6.

Psalm 1 — *Blessed is the man who walks not in the counsel of the wicked, nor stands in the way of sinners, nor sits in the seat of scoffers; but his delight is in the law of the LORD, and on His law he meditates day and night.* **He is like a tree planted by streams of water that yields its fruit in its season, and its leaf does not wither. In all that he does, he prospers.** *The wicked are not so, but are like chaff that the wind drives away. Therefore the wicked will not stand in the judgment, nor sinners in the congregation of the righteous; for the LORD knows the way of the righteous, but the way of the wicked will perish.*

In the third week of our study, we will look at how the blessed man looks as described by the psalmist in verse 3 of the passage.

Verse 3: *He is like a tree planted by streams of water that yields its fruit in its season, and its leaf does not wither. In all that he does, he prospers.*

What are the benefits of a tree that is planted by a stream of water?

_____

_____

_____

_____

Trees need water to survive. In fact, water is the most important nourishment for a tree. The psalmist is making the connection that the man who is blessed is like a tree planted by streams of water. Just as a tree needs water to survive, the Word of God is the most important thing for a believer.

What are the things you need to do in order to be planted in the Word of God? _____

_____

_____

_____

_____

In our society, we have been taught that the key to having a good life is an education. The key to having a good life is having a good job. Or it is this or that. While having an education and a good job are important, true success is only found in the **Word of God**.

How many smart, well-educated people do you know who have miserable lives? _____

_____

_____

_____

_____

When a man is planted in the Word of God, he will bear fruit in his season.

What are some things you would like to see happen in your life as a result of you being planted in the Word of God?

_____

_____

_____

_____

_____

MEMORY SCRIPTURES:

Psalm 1:3: *He is like a tree planted by streams of water that yields its fruit in its season, and its leaf does not wither. In all that he does, he prospers.*

John 15:5-7: *I am the vine; you are the branches. Whoever abides in Me and I in him, he it is that bears much fruit, for apart from Me you can do nothing. If anyone does not abide in Me he is thrown away like a branch and withers; and the branches are gathered, thrown into the fire, and burned. If you abide in Me, and My words abide in you, ask whatever you wish, and it will be done for you.*

CONCLUSION:

The psalmist showed us that a blessed man is like a tree planted by the streams. When we meditate on the Word of God day and night, we, too, become planted by the streams of living waters.

HOMEWORK:

This week write out your plan for how you will stay planted in the Word of God. Write an outline on how you plan on studying Scripture daily.

WHEN IT WAS MY TIME, IT WAS MY TIME.

Ecclesiastes 3:1 — *For everything there is a season, and a time for every matter under heaven.*

It was so frustrating for me. I was doing everything right. I prayed, I read my Bible, I studied. I did everything right. And when I did what was right, I expected results. But nothing was happening. I guess I was like others in our society, I was looking for a quick fix, I wanted to be blessed and blessed *now*. But it seemed like nothing was happening.

I can remember it felt like life was standing still. On the surface it looked like I wasn't blessed. I would see some of my old friends and they seemed to be doing well even though they weren't reading the Bible and following it.

I had to remind myself why I was studying the Bible. I wasn't in it for what I could get or gain. I was in it because, as a born-again believer, I was required to learn the Word of God so I could *live* the Word. I made a promise to myself with tears in my eyes that no matter what may come, I was going to **obey God's Word**.

When it looked like things were standing still, all of a sudden, out of nowhere, *things started happening rapidly*. Relationships were being restored, bad relationships were being replenished, and things were just getting better and better. Finally it all made sense. In Psalm 1:3 it says *in its season*. My season had come, and what a season it has been.

Although things are going much better in my life, I still cherish the days when I had to serve God and walk with Him when I felt like nothing was happening except me learning to obey God. I am all the more grateful for where I am today and know that I am committed to Christ *no matter what.* I can testify to this truth: When it's my season, it's my season. Now I know and fully understand that there truly is a time and a season for everything under the sun.

Inmate Daryl W.

WEEK 4

THE DESCRIPTION OF THE *WICKED* MAN

READ PSALM 1:1-6.

Psalm 1 — *Blessed is the man who walks not in the counsel of the wicked, nor stands in the way of sinners, nor sits in the seat of scoffers; but his delight is in the law of the LORD, and on His law he meditates day and night. He is like a tree planted by streams of water that yields its fruit in its season, and its leaf does not wither. In all that he does, he prospers.* ***The wicked are not so, but are like chaff that the wind drives away.*** *Therefore the wicked will not stand in the judgment, nor sinners in the congregation of the righteous; for the LORD knows the way of the righteous, but the way of the wicked will perish.*

Verse 4: *The wicked are not so, but are like chaff that the wind drives away.*

What are some characteristics that are normally seen in a wicked person? _____

_____

_____

_____

_____

_____

As long as there is a world and people are in it, there will be the wicked. Wicked, evil people are everywhere and they are a part of everyday life. You see it in the news, you see it in the streets, and you see it around you. Wicked people are everywhere.

What is something you can do for the wicked? _____

_____

_____

_____

_____

Chaff is something that is easily driven away. Chaff is weak
and vulnerable. When a person is wicked and is doing evil
deeds, their deeds will not prosper. Nothing they do will last.

Psalm 73:18-19: *Truly You set them in slippery places; You
make them fall to ruin. How they are destroyed in a moment,
swept away utterly by terrors!*

What do you believe makes a person wicked? _____

_____

_____

_____

_____

_____

Why do you believe wicked people normally fellowship with
other wicked people? _____

_____

_____

_____

_____

_____

MEMORY SCRIPTURES:

Psalm 1:4: *The wicked are not so, but are like chaff that the wind drives away.*

Psalm 73:18-19: *Truly You set them in slippery places; You make them fall to ruin. How they are destroyed in a moment, swept away utterly by terrors!*

HOMEWORK:

For this week's homework assignment, write down a person or group of people that were wicked and describe their ruin.

WHATEVER HAPPENED TO THAT GUY?

Psalm 73:18 — *Truly You set them in slippery places; You make them fall to ruin.*

There was a guy I used to know who had it all, or so it seemed. He did what he wanted to do. What he wanted, he got. So many times I would say to myself, "How does this guy get away with this?" OK, I'll be honest — I envied that guy. I didn't want to do the things he did, but I really liked the stuff he had.

I looked at my life and it seemed like I couldn't get a break. Everywhere I turned, something was broken. The only luck I ever had was *bad* luck. The first thing I did that I thought was right turned out to be wrong. And when I did a little wrong, it turned out to be a *huge wrong.* I could not win.

But when I trusted Jesus, it all made sense to me. I was in the place I needed to be. God had always provided for me and what I thought was me being punished was only God chastising me.

One day I asked a close friend of mine what had happened to that guy. What he told me made my mouth drop open. I was very sad to learn that he had died a miserable death. Not only was his death miserable, it was sorrowful. When I heard all of this, I felt convicted by the Holy Spirit for having envied and lusted after a miserable and painful death. I was such a fool.

Today I see the wicked for what they are, **people who need Jesus**. I hope and pray that no one will ever be as foolish and selfish as I was. I should have been praying for that guy and asking for an opportunity to share Jesus with him. Instead, I only envied him and lusted after his position. Now I mourn his awful departure.

Inmate John B.

THE WICKED WILL NOT STAND WITH THE RIGHTEOUS.

READ PSALM 1:1-6.

Psalm 1 — *Blessed is the man who walks not in the counsel of the wicked, nor stands in the way of sinners, nor sits in the seat of scoffers; but his delight is in the law of the LORD, and on His law he meditates day and night. He is like a tree planted by streams of water that yields its fruit in its season, and its leaf does not wither. In all that he does, he prospers. The wicked are not so, but are like chaff that the wind drives away.* **Therefore the wicked will not stand in the judgment, nor sinners in the congregation of the righteous;** *for the LORD knows the way of the righteous, but the way of the wicked will perish.*

Verse 5: *Therefore the wicked will not stand in the judgment, nor sinners in the congregation of the righteous.*

The hand of the Lord will forever be upon the righteous. All throughout the Bible we see that God is faithful to protect and provide for the righteous. The Bible also shows how God deals with the wicked.

There are also times when it appears the wicked are prospering. This can be very frustrating. Many men and women of God have had to witness this and it has led to frustration as it appeared that God wasn't going to judge them.

Explain how you have seen the wicked prosper. _____

_____

_____

_____

_____

Let's look at a couple of verses of Scripture.

Psalm 37:35-36 — *I have seen a wicked, ruthless man, spreading himself like a green laurel tree. But he passed away, and behold, he was no more; though I sought him, he could not be found.*

In verse 35 the psalmist pointed out how the wicked, ruthless man *looked* like he was blessed and prospering. But looks can be deceiving. So many times when a person is wicked it appears that doing the *wrong thing* pays off.

A lot of people engaged in crime because they believed it would pay off. Unfortunately, we all know that doesn't work. Crime doesn't pay. Doing the wrong thing doesn't pay off. Eventually it will catch up with you.

Truth: Doing the *wrong* thing and being *wicked* can **never** lead to a person being blessed.

God is true to His Word. He will deal with the wicked. In verse 36, the psalmist explained the end of the wicked man. He saw him no more, even though he looked for him.

Why do you believe it often looks like the wicked prosper?

_____

_____

_____

_____

_____

_____

How does it make you feel when you see the wicked getting ahead in life as a result of doing wrong things? _____

_____

_____

_____

_____

_____

_____

It's very frustrating when we see the wicked getting ahead for doing the wrong things. But it is an illusion. God is faithful to His Word and, above all, God is faithful to honor those who do what is right. When a man reads the Word of God and *does* it, that man will be blessed and will prosper. He will bring forth his fruit in his *season* accordingly. The question is no longer *if*, it is *when*. This is very important to understand. We are all guilty of wanting quick fixes. God doesn't work like that. God works within His own timing. Therefore, don't be discouraged. Continue to stay planted in the Word of God, *no matter what!*

Why do you believe the wicked will not be able to stand in the judgment of God? _____

_____

_____

_____

_____

_____

What will you do when you feel discouraged and you don't see anything happening in your life? _____

_____

_____

_____

_____

_____

_____

_____

Notes:

MEMORY SCRIPTURES:

Psalm 1:5-6: *Therefore the wicked will not stand in the judgment, nor sinners in the congregation of the righteous. For the LORD knows the way of the righteous, but the way of the wicked will perish.*

Psalm 73:16-17: *But when I thought how to understand this, it seemed to me a wearisome task, until I went into the sanctuary of God; then I discerned their wend.*

CONCLUSION:

Psalm 1 makes it very clear to us what it takes to be blessed. If a man heeds the instructions written in these verses and applies them to his daily life, he will be blessed. In order to be blessed, we must learn to position ourselves and do what the Lord says. Ultimately, we must become doers of the Word, not only hearers of the Word (James 1:22).

When we are beginning our journey towards heeding the Word of God, we must remember why we are doing it. We follow the Lord because it is man's duty to obey God. There is no greater joy and honor than to please and satisfy our heavenly Father. Although there may be benefits that come with being blessed and living a righteous life, we must always remain true to why we do it. We do it because of the love we have for our God.

THEY DON'T KNOW GOD.

At first I didn't think there was much of a difference between myself, a Christian, and a person who didn't know the Lord. I really didn't see the difference.

It wasn't until I started to see how my life was going and noticed that I often said, "Boy, was I lucky!" or "That was a close call." I also kept seeing how the wicked were falling to the wayside over and over again. When I would look in the cell blocks, I kept seeing the same guys in the same blocks. They would get out and then get right back in.

One day it finally dawned on me. I had also been caught in the same cycle as those men once. And the reason for the cycle was simple, **I didn't know God**. Because I didn't know Him, I was constantly being judged and punished for my inappropriate behavior each time I violated the rules.

The wicked cannot stand in the judgment of God because they don't know what it takes to please God. They don't know the Word of God, which shows the will of God. Therefore, they can't and won't ever be able to stand. I am very happy to say that I know I can stand because I am no longer a wicked man, I am the righteousness of Christ Jesus.

Inmate Kenneth M.

GOD PREPARES THE WAY OF THE RIGHTEOUS.

READ PSALM 1:1-6.

Psalm 1 — *Blessed is the man who walks not in the counsel of the wicked, nor stands in the way of sinners, nor sits in the seat of scoffers; but his delight is in the law of the LORD, and on His law he meditates day and night. He is like a tree planted by streams of water that yields its fruit in its season, and its leaf does not wither. In all that he does, he prospers. The wicked are not so, but are like chaff that the wind drives away. Therefore the wicked will not stand in the judgment, nor sinners in the congregation of the righteous;* **for the LORD knows the way of the righteous, but the way of the wicked will perish.**

Verse 6: *For the LORD knows the way of the righteous, but the way of the wicked will perish.*

In our final week and our final verse, we are going to discover another benefit of the blessed man. That benefit is that God watches over the righteous man's way. I can remember when as a young child my parents watched over me. Even now I can still remember the peace I had knowing that my parents had my back as I played in the park or the yard. I would occasionally look to see if they were still watching, and when I looked, they were there. That taught me so much about their love and concern for me.

What is greater than the Lord watching over the righteous? Absolutely nothing.

In your own words, explain how God is watching over your way.

_____

_____

_____

_____

_____

What are some of the benefits that come from the Lord watching over the righteous? _____

_____

_____

_____

Wouldn't it be amazing if we had the same abilities as our heavenly Father? If we could be *all-knowing*, *all-powerful*, and *all-present*, I believe we, too, would watch over the way of the people we love and care for.

Why would you want to watch over the way of someone you love? _____

_____

_____

_____

The last part of verse 6 informs us that *the way of the wicked will perish.*

Why do you believe the way of the wicked will perish? _____

_____

_____

_____

_____

MEMORY SCRIPTURES:

Proverbs 10:25: *When the tempest passes, the wicked is no more, but the righteous is established forever.*

Psalm 37:18: *The LORD knows the days of the blameless, and their heritage will remain forever.*

CONCLUSION:

All throughout the Bible it is clear that God will forever take care of the righteous. In time, the wicked will perish. This is the way and the will of God. He will provide special care for the righteous and not for the wicked.

What is there to be learned from Psalm 1? There are benefits from abiding in the Word of God. Righteous men study and meditate on the Word and as a result, they are blessed. Likewise, the wicked neither meditate nor study God's Word and they are not blessed.

The blessed man is blessed because he *obeys* the Word of God. The wicked man is *cursed* because he doesn't know God.

HOMEWORK:

By now you should have memorized all of Psalm 1 and the other memory verses. The challenge for you is to now challenge someone close to you to also memorize those Scriptures. Take what you have learned and share it with others. You know that you *own* something when you can teach it. If you can teach it, it belongs to you.

HE WAS ALWAYS THERE.

The greatest loss I have ever experienced was the passing of my father when I was 7 years old. He had made me feel special. I knew he loved me and knew he always had my back. When I lost him, I wondered who would watch over me like my father had. For years, this question pressed on me. I wanted someone to have my back.

As the years passed, my life consisted of people coming in my life and leaving my life. That was my story. I had *no* stability. I was looking for a love like my father's in all the wrong places. I thought if I hung out with *these* guys, they would watch my back. *They didn't.* I thought if I had *this* person in my life, they would watch my back. But no one did. When I used to remember the experiences I had, I would become depressed.

I found myself in a cell in 2001 and I thought I was alone. I was wrong. Not only was there someone in the cell with me, He had made it known to me that He had been there the entire time. When I gave my life to Jesus and started to grow in the grace and knowledge of who He was and is, it hit me, the whole time He was there. When things went wrong, He was there. Things that should have killed me couldn't because He was there. He was watching over me the whole time.

It's not a fact, it's a truth. God watches over the righteous. God watches over me because of His promise that He will never leave nor forsake me. Today it is very evident and plain to see that God has been and continues to watch over my way.

Inmate George G.

MORE FROM LIFELINE GLOBAL MINISTRIES™

Malachi Dads™ and Hannah's Gift™ programs are in prisons and jails throughout the United States and internationally. Lifeline Global Ministries™ helps to restore and equip incarcerated men and women to become godly parents so that the generational cycle of incarceration can be broken. *To find out how you can order Lifeline Global Ministries™ curriculum, please visit the website at www.lifelineglobal.org.*

Malachi Dads™ — The Heart of a Father
This 12-week curriculum for men's prison ministry provides practical biblical advice for life, marriage and parenting. Quickly growing as a significant force in fathering, the Malachi Dads™ program is designed for fathers in the most broken of places — prison. It shows men how to become Christ-followers and grow in their faith. *Also available in Spanish.*

Malachi Dads™ — The Heart of a Man - Part 1
This 12-lesson study teaches incarcerated fathers how they can have a heart that pleases God, regardless of their past sins. Helps fathers in prison understand what it means to be men after God's own heart. This Malachi Dads™ study has memory verses and assignments. Topics cover trustworthiness, temptations and purity, prayer and more. *Also available in Spanish.*

Malachi Dads™ — The Heart of a Man - Part 2
Continue The Heart of a Man study with new lessons that address how to develop godly character and integrity in your walk with God. Includes lessons designed to help men live as godly examples in their families and communities. This curriculum for men's prison ministry provides practical, biblical advice for life, marriage and parenting. *Also available in Spanish.*

Malachi Dads™ — Family Restoration
Powerful lessons based on the book of Jeremiah that teach incarcerated fathers about healthy communication, authority, the promise of restoration and more.

Malachi Dads™ — Inmate Challenge DVD

This DVD component of the Malachi Dads™ Heart of a Father curriculum was filmed on location at the famed Angola Prison in Louisiana. Three inmate fathers share their stories and their challenge to other inmates. This DVD is an ideal launching point for jail or prison ministry and for challenging fathers to consider the legacy they are leaving. Includes a five-week small group discussion guide. *To order your copy of the Inmate Challenge DVD, visit the Lifeline Global Ministries™ website: www.lifelinegobal.org, or your Lifeline mentor.*

Hannah's Gift™ — Psalm 23

This powerful six-lesson devotional helps you reflect on the many ways God is always with us as our Shepherd, our Peace, our Provider, our Victory, our Righteousness and our Healer. Written by inmates at Louisiana Correctional Institution for Women who are taking part in the Hannah's Gift™ prison ministry, each lesson includes a personal testimony and brief devotional, discussion questions and verses to memorize.

Hannah's Gift™ — The Heart of a Mother

Hannah's Gift™ is a 12-week program especially for women's prison ministry. The Heart of a Mother is modeled after the life of Hannah and her son as told in the first two chapters of 1 Samuel in the Old Testament. This curriculum offers mothers the opportunity to parent from a distance and give a legacy of faith to their children. Also available in Spanish.

Hannah's Gift™ — Family Restoration

This study provides incarcerated mothers biblical steps for building healthy family relationships straight from God's Word. This powerful, easy-to-follow devotional has 10 lessons from the book of Jeremiah. Each lesson includes a memory verse and five days' worth of study materials, devotionals and assignments. Topics include healthy communication, authority, and the promise of restoration.

Hannah's Gift™ — Beautiful Woman

This book identifies key struggles that trip women up and cause them to forfeit their happiness and joy. It helps women to see that the rules they have been playing by will lead to defeat. It will show them a better way out of their chaos through the truth of God's Word. These 10 lessons are designed to help women find their place as Beautiful Women in this world.

Equip Leaders

This easy-to-follow guide trains Malachi Dads™ and Hannah's Gift™ facilitators to effectively lead inmate small groups. Each chapter gives readers key verses, biblical foundations, methods, teaching pointers and more for leading small groups. Topics include ministry for life change, hand on the Word, and gospel of grace. *Also available in Spanish.*

ORDER TODAY!

To find out how you can order Lifeline Global Ministries™ curriculum, please visit the website at **www.lifelineglobal.org**

THE MALACHI DADS PLEDGE:

As a Malachi Dad, I solemnly pledge to glorify God and build His kingdom by prioritizing the raising of godly children, first in my family, then in the influencing of other men to do the same in theirs. I firmly believe that my transformed life in Christ — my life of integrity, pursuit of this vision, and the pursuit of godly character — will allow me to impact my children, family and others towards this end.

I will practice a life of daily discipline and dependence on God through prayer and the study of God's Word for the wisdom in how to "nurture my children in the admonition of the Lord." I will pursue this endeavor for a lifetime whether my children are in my home or not.

Finally, I believe that my end goal is not only for my children to walk in the Lord but this God-given vision would impact multiple generations to come.

So help me God.

70909954R00033

Made in the USA
Columbia, SC
24 August 2019